THE DEFINITIVE GUIDE for becoming
THE WORLD'S GREATEST AUNT OR

UNCLE!

WILL MURRAY

NEW YORK

UNCLE
The Definitive Guide for Becoming the World's Greatest Aunt or Uncle

by Will Murray
© 2011 Will Murray. All rights reserved.

ISBN 978-1-60037-946-8 Paperback
ISBN 978-1-60037-947-5 E-Pub
Library of Congress Control Number: 2011922092

Published by:

MORGAN JAMES PUBLISHING
The Entrepreneurial Publisher
5 Penn Plaza, 23rd Floor
New York City, New York 10001
(212) 655-5470 Office
(516) 908-4496 Fax
www.MorganJamesPublishing.com

Interior Design by:
Bonnie Bushman
bbushman@bresnan.net

In an effort to support local communities, raise awareness and funds, Morgan James Publishing donates one percent of all book sales for the life of each book to Habitat for Humanity.
Get involved today, visit
www.HelpHabitatForHumanity.org.

For aunts and uncles,
and the twinkle in their eyes.

CONTENTS

ILLUSTRATIONS

PROLOGUE

"Every wild apple shrub excites our expectations thus somewhat as every wild child. It is, perhaps, a prince in disguise. What a lesson to man!"

—Thoreau

Anytime you go into a bookstore, you can find about a truckload of books on parenting. Parenting the gifted child. Parenting the willful child. Parenting twins. Parenting the average child. But you won't find a single volume on how to be an aunt or an uncle. Not one. Oh, sure, you might see a couple of sentimental odes to the Aunt. But nothing about how to go about "aunting." And this oversight needs attention.

Aunts and uncles have always had a very special place in the development of humanity, and their role is growing increasingly vital.

1

UNCLE

Parents have a thoroughly identified role. Spawn the kid, feed it, clothe it, house it, send it to school, keep it alive, and nag it incessantly.

Grandparents have a special role—spoil, spoil, spoil. "Hi honey, you want a cookie?" "Won't you have a little more dessert?" "Do you need us to buy you anything?" "Oh, don't be so tough on her—she's just a child!" And on and on. Well done.

But aunts and uncles, the invisible bearers of human culture, the unsung heroes of the development of good human beings, can be found nowhere on the radar screen.

Some parents, many parents, maybe almost all parents, don't want their kids to act like kids. Let's face it—kids can be a pain. They make more noise than machines that shear metal. They find dirt and make messes where none exists. They create entropy. They take apart things that should be together and put things together that should remain apart. They mix salt and sugar, water and soil. They would mix nitro and glycerin if they could get their hands on it.

Kids find danger in the safest of places and create it if it isn't lying about. They work hard at trying to get killed. They search for broken glass to eat, electric sockets to poke metal objects into, and cliffs to fall from. As if by magic, they hone in on "The Place Where They Can Do The Most Damage."

A colleague at work has three wonderful kids. They came into the office one day with their mom—a fun outing. The youngest, Amy, instantly sized up the office treasures: staplers, tape, top-heavy file cabinets, carefully arranged documents on the desk, pushpins, letter opener, Swiss army knife, telephone. Then she headed straight for the computer keyboard, arms outstretched and fingers wiggling. If I hadn't headed her off, I'm certain the random keystrokes she'd have made would have resulted in this sequence:

```
<<Format hard drive?>>

Y.

<<Are you sure?>>

Y.

<<All data will be lost. Forever.
Irretrievably. We're not kidding. Are
you still sure???>>

Y.
```

So parents have a real reason for wanting their kids to act like miniature adults. It's just not a good reason. Dress them up cute, but don't let them create messes, wail like banshees, find the lipstick, hide the car keys, fingerpaint the wall with shoe polish, write their names on the cat with bleach, or take all the CD jewel cases from the stereo cabinet and build forts with them. You see, parents don't really want kids; they want harmless tiny adults—ones they can get to do what they want (unlike every single one of the full-sized adults they have to contend with every day).

This is where aunts and uncles enter the fracas. If parents got their wish, how would these little bitty adults grow up? I say: miserably. Into accountants probably. Or worse than that, economists (defined by some—not me of course—as accountants without personality). Humorless, dour, sour, serious, and generally un-fun to be around. To become an adult human being worthy of the title, you must be allowed to be a child when you are a child. The dough must be allowed to rise.

Aunts and uncles have a unique and indispensable role in creating a human race that will be up to the task of living well on the planet. It is we, the aunts and uncles, who must help kids learn how to be children. Nobody else will do it. They need to know how to chew food and show it to people on their wildly protruding tongues, blow bubbles, tell knock-knock jokes badly, and make cow and chicken sounds.

The ideas in this book provide a start! You won't find every kid-thing in the world in here or every kind of kid-skill to impart. In writing this book, I stayed away from including activities that are dangerous, evil, or just plain mean. The world is full of human cussedness already, and we certainly need less of it. Kids can do mean things, but they can also learn not to do them.

Use your judgment here. If you feel your sibling's kid is too young for any of the "tricks" you'll read about, save it for later or just use restraint.

Enjoy all the fun things for your nieces and nephews you'll find in this book. They're for you, too. And by the way, when was the last time you came home with grass stains on the knees of your jeans?

MAJOR TIMES AND THINGS IN KIDS' LIVES

Kids' lives can be full of exuberance or full of drudgery, nothing but excitement or nothing but boredom, amazingly joyous or dull, dull, dull.

As an aunt or uncle, you may recall flashes of times here and there, hints of what it was like when you—yes you, yourself—were young.

- Your 10,000-volt anticipation of the end of school and beginning of summer vacation;

- Your exuberance when the older kids let you tag along;

- The first time you were allowed a tiny sip of beer and how stunned you were that it looked like crème soda but didn't taste anything like crème soda.

Kids growing up have major events in their lives that are often measured in tiny increments that tend to slide by you now. The little things hold a lot of meaning for a kid who sees them as big things.

This book reveals eight main categories of life that affect kids. For each category, you'll find hints on how you, as an aunt or uncle, can play a significant role in the lives of your nieces and nephews.

Traveling is a big thing, not only because of its opportunities for zaniness, but also because it's a major time sink for an awful lot of kids. They spend much their day sitting in a car getting carried from one house to another, one school to another, one sporting match to another, one music lesson to another. For them, traveling can be a bore. *You* can save them from staring at their game console or tiny little video screen. Yes, *you* can liven up that part of their lives.

Food looms large in a kid's day. Breakfast, we all know, is the most important meal of the day, along with lunch, dinner, and also snacks. Clint Eastwood once said that he can tell what any dog is thinking. That dog is thinking: "I'm hungry." Kids, alas, are quite the same—always hungry. Food is cause for celebrating as well as fueling, for respectful fun as well as nutrition, joy as well as maintenance. You can help bring out the fun side of food.

Words can be the source of fun, cleverness, and rapport, and can also be educational. "Word play" is called "play" for a reason. Jokes, puns, and commentaries (aka smart remarks) are readily available to serve in your arsenal of entertaining activities.

Animals seem to innately fascinate kids. Some people say that kids learn how to distinguish between similar things by telling animals apart. Making fine distinctions proves to be an important skill. For example, it comes in handy to know the difference between rock candy and mothballs when you have a sweet tooth, or in a far earlier time, between the domesticated wolf and the saber-toothed tiger padding in your direction. Kids have a penchant for animals, *and* they can be tough on them without a little guidance. You can be the guide.

Special days present opportunities for interaction. Although you can make any day special, some days offer bigger occasions than others. Named holidays—Halloween, Thanksgiving, the Fourth of July (stuffily, Independence Day)—are wonderful excuses to go see your nephews and nieces and get reacquainted with them. Other days are special in their own way. The day the cousins come to visit— special. The day you come to visit—special again.

And whatever you can do to make any old ordinary day special, well, do it!

Things you just must do can be high on your list. These are things kids need to experience or know about and things they have to see. What things? To name only a few: having contests to find out who can remain silent the longest, impersonating things or animals, and swinging on gates. It's up to you and your imagination.

Just hanging out approaches the status of art form for kids. You can do plenty of things to make spending time together memorable. Your nieces and nephews revere you. You can do the simplest things with them and just by being with them make these events indelible in their memories and lives.

Toys, tricks, and trial balloons round out the major categories of experience for youth. Along their life path, they need to learn how to launch a rubber band, turn almost any hollow vessel into a drum, or figure out how many different ways to use a paper cup. Who else will teach them such skills? You can fill the gap.

Now let's get you set up with the specifics.

TIPS FOR TRAVELING

Traveling, whether by car or bus or train or plane, takes up a lot of kids' time. They travel to school. They travel to sports and dance and science camp. They travel to visit relatives. They travel so much that the miracle of modern transportation becomes a bore.

Not so long ago, a trip across the Great Plains was fraught with peril—heat, drought, wind, locusts, rattlesnakes, and hail the size of Volkswagens. And kids had to *walk*. On that journey, people suffered and people died. By the wagonload.

These days, in a plane, we traverse the Great Plains in only two and a half hours, and, in a car, in only a day. Hardships still abound, for certain. The person in seat 24A in front of your niece reclines his seat so far that he might as well introduce himself.

And a day-long car trip, *one whole day* can seem like torture.

It doesn't have to be this way. You can make transportation a fun experience. The activities below, listed in alphabetical order so you can browse through them quickly, give you ideas about how to prevent the miracle of modern transportation from becoming the Donner Party.

Cars. A big topic. More and more, kids spend a lot of time in cars. A lot. So, what to do when you're in the car with them? First, turn off the video if the car has one. Too passive, this electronic babysitter. Then take the lead on these ideas:

Questions. Using your best whiny voice, ask, "When are we going to be there? How much longer? How many **minutes**?" See if you can get a chorus of whining, the whinier the better. Turn up and turn down the volume. Left side of the car then right side. Girls versus boys. Front seat versus back seat. It's extremely difficult to be grumpy and whiny when you are laughing hard enough to crack a rib.

Passing up the restaurants is also good fun. Notice a roadside restaurant and casually remark how good the fries are in McDonald's or the pizza is at Pizza Hut or the chicken sandwiches at Burger King. "Ooooh, McDonald's—it has the *best* fries." When the kids burst out demanding to stop and get some, just as casually say, "We've already gone past. We missed the exit. Too late. Oh, well. We'll just have to keep going." Then repeat with the next restaurant. "Ooooh, Wendy's. It has the *best* chocolate milkshakes." Stop before you create a mutiny.

Punch buggies (Volkswagen Beetles), out-of-state license plates, and related observational activities, always create sure-fire fun. Pick out something that kids would see or hear once in a while on the road and call it out. Yellow taxis , convertibles, cars with license plates from other states. See who can call them out first. It's an ancient pastime (in the automobile age) that has staying power because it works.

Magic turn signals. In a sly way, activate the turn indicator then remark to your nephew, "Hey, the turn signal came on telling us *to turn right*. Guess we need to turn right here. Pretty smart car, huh? If you happen to have a GPS system, they really are smart. They actually *tell* you where to turn. Demonstrate amazement when the GPS knows what to do ahead of time. *"How did it do that?"*

Crosswalks. Mimic the Walking Man icon on the crosswalk signal—all the way across the street.

Gifts. Little presents delight kids at any time. That crinkly packet of four and a half broken pretzels you got from the flight attendant on your airplane trip there? Good gift. Bring a little present every time you visit.

Hand maps. Hands are versatile props. In addition to making rabbits on the projector screen, hands can form windshield wipers. Thumbs can detach. Fingers can be double jointed. Everyone from Michigan knows that your hand makes a map of the state. California, too. Cup your hands together, palms up.

Tips for Traveling

Your palms represent the Great Central Valley, your fingers the mighty Sierra Nevada mountains, your left thumb lofty Mt. Shasta, higher than 14,000 feet, and your right thumb the Tehachapi Range north of Los Angeles. Your wrist is the coastline, and the gaps between your fingers are California's major rivers (from the north: Yuba, Pit, American, Stanislaus, Tuolumne, Merced, Kings, Kern, and Tule.)

Your right hand can easily shape a map of the San Francisco Bay Area. If you live in Houston or Indianapolis or anywhere else, you'll just have to figure this one out on your own.

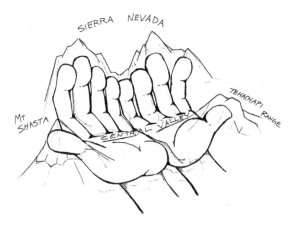

Hay. When you're driving down the road and pass a truck full of hay or a field of hay, whoever sees it first shouts "HAAAAY!!" at the top of their lungs. Once everyone has been thoroughly startled, that person calmly points to the hay. Everyone in the car will jump a foot, even with seat belts on. At least the driver won't get drowsy again for a while.

Kicking the seatback in front of you. I don't know why kids absolutely must do this in a car or an airplane, but they do. Good for you that it isn't something you need to teach them. They have this ability from birth. But you *can* teach them to knock it off. First, ask your nephew very nicely to keep his feet off the seatback in front of him. If that doesn't do trick, ask him if you should change seats with the person behind him, so that you can kick the back of *his* seat.

Limousines. Passengers in limousines know that the smoked window glass means they can't be seen by mere pedestrians and people in more humble vehicles, like prison buses and Dodge Darts. So I like to wave at them to make them wonder that we really *can* see them—and that what they've been doing is readily transparent to everyone along their path. Get your siblings' kids to give an enthusiastic wave in tandem with a friendly, "Hey!! How ya doin'?" It will give the limousine passengers a little something to think about.

Riding bicycles. If your niece isn't riding a bike yet, get her on one. The bicycle is the most efficient form of human transportation ever invented in terms of calorie burn per mile. Bicycles are fast, fun, safe, and more—plus they mean freedom. Once a kid has a bike and reasonable permission to go, she feels free! So ride with her. Teach her the rules of the road, how to corner (point your chin where you want the bike to go and slightly lean into the turn) and how to stay clear of the cars. While you're out riding, tell her to look down the road apiece and pretend that you and she are flying free, four feet off the ground. *We are freeeeeeee!*

Road signs. By necessity, road signs are terse. The letters have to be large enough for the driver to read at driving speed, so the number of words has a strict limit. Being terse, road signs are subject to various interpretations like these:

UNCLE

You see a wide orange sign proclaiming "End Construction." Agree with it; we have too much development already.

Your niece will not dispute you when you talk about the yellow "End School Zone" sign. Everybody can agree we should have zones in which we End School.

I'm always saddened by signs that say "Slow children at play." I guess everyone can't be an Einstein.

Pedestrian X-ing, why are they "X"-ing the pedestrians?

Everybody knows the red hexagonal stop sign, but this sign is never, ever fully obeyed. Why? Because after drivers stop at that sign (or do what passes for a stop), then they go again. The sign doesn't say "Stop, then if the coast is clear, go on ahead." It just says, "Stop." So, obey the sign until the drivers behind you give nonverbal cues that it's time to go and your nephew is begging you to hit the gas.

FOOD FOR MAXIMUM IMPACT

This category is limited only by your creativity.

Lookies. To get you started, consider that chewing food and showing it to others is one of a kid's essential joys in life. Some call it "See Food" or "Lookies" because you say to the intended viewer, "Lookie, lookie." That attracts his attention so you can show off what you're chewing.

Food items for maximum Lookie impact are mixed vegetables, French fries with ketchup, and Oreo cookies if you show them just after you've broken them up but before the pieces are homogenized. Granted, you want to use Lookies only in safe situations, like when everyone else at the table is goofing off. In restaurants, with company and at the homes of their friends and grandparents—probably never.

Big bites. The outline of a nice big bite in a sandwich is a thing of beauty. Bite large, then be proud. Show it off to anyone who will notice.

Food in teeth. This blight need not be a source of embarrassment; it can be great fun. Smile a lot after eating corn on the cob, barbecued ribs, poppy seed rolls, or broccoli. It's easy to make a game of it. As with Lookies, do this only when the situation demands it. Dinner at your niece's grandfather doesn't demand it.

Gum. Offering someone ABC gum is a fun thing to do. ABC, of course, means "Already Been Chewed." Almost no one accepts the offer once they understand what you're offering. Then you have the disposal problem. By the time you're 43 years old, you've learned to save the wrapper to put the dead gum in. But this requires planning and forethought, which most of us haven't got. We throw the gum wrapper away as soon as we pop the gum into our mouths. Sticking the bland, tired gum under a desk, table, or chair is harmless (depending on the value of the furniture to its owner, who will eventually discover it—you hope long enough after the affixation that the suspect could be anybody) but it's behavior that's beneath you. The best thing is to spit or place it into the garbage can (see entry titled **Seeds, spitting**).

Helping in the kitchen. Your nieces and nephews want to "help" in the kitchen. They really do mean it as help. In terms of culinary efficiency, though, their help is a dead loss. So what? Life's not all about efficiency, as though we were manufacturing computer chips. It's about fun. It's also about fulfillment, about being together doing something, about spilling messy things like honey and flour, about doing new activities, about creating something, and about food. And it's about teaching kids how to read a recipe—that there *is* such a thing as a recipe. Helping in the kitchen can be a perfect storm of great things. Encourage it. Say yes. Delegate. And find a way to work *molasses* into the recipe.

Hiding under the table. At dinner (the more formal the better), when someone leaves the table for any reason, have everyone hide under the table. When the absentee returns, keep the giggling down and act completely innocent.

Ice-cream-headache dance. When you eat too much ice cream too fast, you get an ice-cream headache. To make it go away, teach your neice to do the ice-cream-headache dance. It goes like this: Stamp up and down rapidly on your feet while holding your hands, arms bent like chicken wings, in front of you at shoulder height, and waving them forward and back in short, rapid strokes, as if you were flying with only your hands. This dance actually doesn't help your ice-cream headache to go away any faster, but everyone does it so you should, too.

Ketchup. It's weird food. It looks like blood. Point out to your nephew that ketchup comes from the tomato, which is actually a fruit, not a vegetable. And what about the squeeze bottle? What could be more fun than to write your name in ketchup on your plate?

Orange peel teeth. A classic. Quarter a medium-sized orange and separate the peel. Make an incision down the middle two-thirds of the way along the length of the peel slice, then make three or four short cuts across the first incision. Turn the peel inside out and insert it behind your lips and in front of your teeth. Move to the mirror and behold the masterpiece. Stick out your tongue through the teeth for added effect.

Pancake art. Pancake batter pours easily and sets up terrifically, which makes it ideal for art projects. Sure, you can shape it into bunnies and Mickey Mouse, caterpillars, stars, and snowmen. You get the picture.

Popcorn. No explanation necessary. Enjoy it often, especially when your niece gets to help pop it. "Hey, *I* know. Let's make...*popcorn*."

Food for Maximum Impact

Restaurant behavior. In all seriousness, your nephews and nieces need to have restaurant etiquette, especially if they dine out only occasionally. This behavior transfers to eating at the homes of their friends. When their friends' parents report how nicely behaved they were at dinner, your siblings will wonder who they're talking about. "Can't be *our* kids!"

Some basic rules: Use utensils from the outside in, stick the napkin in your lap as soon as you sit down, notice what other people are doing and if it looks right, do it too. Chew. Eat then talk, but not both at the same time.

Teach them how to calculate a tip and how the tip is important to the servers' finances (servers get most of their income from tips and the restaurant pays them peanuts). Be crazy and, once in a while, tip before ordering. (TIPS is a long-lost acronym for "to ensure proper service" and historically, the patron did indeed tip up front.) And always, always, always be polite to the restaurant staff—from the hostess to the bus boy.

Be prepared to recover from restaurant mishaps. Spills happen, and their cleanup also happens. No big deal; be comforting and shrug it off. Unless you are the spiller. Then you can laugh it off.

UNCLE

Kids sometimes say unfortunate things in restaurants, such as when my niece Jeanine observed the refried beans on the lady's plate at the next table and asked, "Why does that lady's dinner look like diarrhea?" Well, there's no good answer to that, at least right away. The lady didn't think so either and picked around at her plate for a few minutes before pushing it away.

Seeds. Seeds offer a wealth of opportunities. Orange, apple, and grape seeds make excellent spitting projectiles. Accuracy and distance contests provide a great way to while away the time and a chance to build skills that kids will thank you for later in life.

Watermelon seeds deserve special mention. Sleek, shiny, slippery, and flat, spitting watermelon seeds can provide a lesson in physics. Besides that, it's about as much fun as fun can be. Let's face it, when you're eating watermelon, you're already a mess (unless you're eating it with a fork, which is just wrong). You have watermelon juice running down your chin and dripping down your wrists if you're doing it right. So go all the way and spit. The watermelon seed's aerodynamic shape makes it a good traveler.

But wait; it gets better. While your hands are nice and moist, squeeze a seed between your thumb and index finger. Watch where you aim it. For distance, nothing can beat watermelon seeds. For accuracy, well, they're a little unpredictable. Here's where the physics comes in.

Remember vectors from introductory physics and trigonometry? (What? You forgot all that stuff as soon as you finished the final exam?) Vectors are physical forces in different directions that combine to one overall force. Why, when you pinch the seed between thumb and finger, does it travel 90 degrees to the direction of the force? Vectors. Can you teach physics to kids using watermelon seeds? Sure, but it's more fun to put a piece of paper on the wall and shoot for bull's eyes.

Sharing. Sharing is good. Share every chance you get. Demonstrably, casually, however you want, say, "Here, you want some of this?" Civilization can't continue without social eating—and without sharing its fruits.

Snacks. This item might best belong in the grandparents' manual, but you can use it, too. Kids can always eat. Offering them food ensures continuing interest and loyalty. Fun snacks with colored sprinkles or some other off-the-wall addition keeps kids happy for at least a few minutes.

Spills. Inevitable and unavoidable, spills don't have to be a cause for dismay. Surely, the tablecloth will wash, the floor will mop, the carpet will clean (unless it's a white carpet, and then the carpet owners deserve what they get). Spills are common enough that their inconvenience shouldn't be an obstacle to having a little fun with them.

Sometimes, an *absence* of spills can bring tension to the dinner atmosphere. At one of our family's Thanksgiving dinners, the buzz got around among the 29 diners that no one had yet spilled a beverage on the dining table, and this was unusual. Gradually, everyone tensed up and conversation faded. The atmosphere thickened with worry. Nobody wanted to be the one to spill. Finally, my brother Jim nonchalantly knocked over his water glass and said, "There. Everyone can relax now." So we did.

Straw wrappers. Paper wrappers on drinking straws make great missiles when you leave most of the wrapper on the straw then blow hard. But then go retrieve it. You just don't want to litter.

WHACKY WORD PLAY

Words are wonderful. Always around, abundant, free, and entertaining, words are the best "toys" we have. Nothing to do? Play a word game. Nothing to give? Tell a joke. Nowhere to go? Invent a huge and important secret right where you are. Almost terminally bored? Pretend to be a sports announcer and describe in electron-microscope detail everything that's not happening.

Try these ideas and you'll be amazed at your nieces' and nephews' quick wits and facility with words. Revel with them.

Play-by-play announcing. Play-by-play announcers of sporting events have a good time. They get to broadcast what's happening in a game to people who aren't at the game as it happens. Let's face it; many people aren't in the game of life; they either watch it as if it were on television or drift through it in a fog.

Try this: Have your young charges describe what's happening around them as if they were play-by-play announcers. "He's walking toward the salad bar, grabs a plate, looks left, spies the lettuce. He's going for the tongs! *He's got the lettuce!*" Then add color to the event (like the TV "color commentators" who complement the play-by-play announcer). "Gee that's right, Bob, it's lettuce alright." Doing this sharpens the kids' powers of observation, plus watching people in that kind of detail is just plain entertaining.

Do this: Announce the emerging action in that announcer voice and then get your niece or nephew to take over. "Mom is heading for the stove with a pot of water. She checks to the side to see if she left the water running. Steps in front of the range. Sets the pot on the left front burner. Now she's reaching for the knob, checks over her shoulder to see why we are talking like this. Shakes her head, goes back to the knob. She's cranking the knob, and...and...yes, the stove lights! *Score for Mom!*"

Conduct the post-game interview if you like, complete with hackneyed one-liners uttered by breathless athletes. Don't forget gems like these:

"We came to play."

"They are a very fine ballclub."

"We just got some breaks today."

"You have to play one game at a time."

"Couldn't do it without the team."

Being overheard. While in a restaurant or another public place where you will be overheard, say something like this:

"What are shoes made of?"

"Hide."

"Why should I hide?"

"Hide! Hide, a cow's outside."

"I'm not going to hide from a bunch of cows."

"Herd."

"Heard of what?"

"Herd of cows."

"Sure I've heard of cows. What's your point?"

Figures of speech. Sayings in everyday use are fun, especially when twisted in odd, Yogi Berra kinds of ways. Take those that sound okay to the ear but don't come out on paper exactly the same, so to speak (or is it soda-speak?).

Right from the gecko. (Get go? What *is* a get-go?)

Take it for granite. (Careful, it's heavy.)

What a wino. (What do I know? I dunno.)

Sadly the cross-eyed bear. (What cross, and who asked you to bear it?)

More on. Moron is not a nice name to call anybody, so don't let it happen. First, there's the matter of pronunciation. Whether you say it like a two-part first name (Moe Ron) or not doesn't matter. When somebody says, "I want ketchup so I can put some moron my fries," gently remind that person that it's not nice to say "moron" and leave it at that.

Quiet. Being unusually quiet positively unnerves parents. But timing is key. Pick a time when the 'rents are a little distracted and then get everybody hushed up. Wait. Be patient. Someone will soon come snooping around, puzzled or frightened.

Silence contests are also easy to instigate fun, especially if the prize is appealing. "I'll bet you a quarter you can't be quiet for two minutes." I'll bet they can't either.

Quotations. Somebody has already said just what you need to say, only better. So, go ahead and quote that person. Here are some favorites that your niece will appreciate, or least puzzle over.

"It's a no-brainer, if you just think about it." Alan Carpenter

Yogi Berra's quotations are legendary. About a restaurant, *"Nobody goes there anymore. It's too crowded."* And *"50 percent of baseball is 90 percent mental."*

Late in his life, when presented with a difficult question, Albert Einstein is said to have replied, *"I'm no Einstein."*

"Whatever you can do, or dream you can, begin it. Boldness has genius, power, and magic in it." Goethe

"Let us endeavor so to live that when we come to die even the undertaker will be sorry." Mark Twain

"My life has been filled with terrible misfortunes—most of which never happened." Mark Twain

"If you don't know where you are going, you might end up somewhere else." Yogi Berra

"It's not worthy of a human being to give up." Sissella Bok

"The first law of garbage: everybody wants you to pick it up, and nobody wants you to put it down." William Ruckelshaus

"Nobody makes a greater mistake than he who did nothing because he could only do a little." Edmund Burke

"If you want to do something, do it. You can always make it better later." John Stevens, builder of the Panama Canal

"Imagination is more important than knowledge." Albert Einstein

"You miss 100 percent of the shots you never take." Wayne Gretzky

"Be kind. Remember everyone you meet is fighting an uphill battle." T.H. Thompson

"Nothing great is ever accomplished without enthusiasm." Ralph Waldo Emerson

"You must do the thing you think you cannot do." Eleanor Roosevelt

"Losers visualize the penalties of failure. Winners visualize the rewards of success." Rob Gilbert

"Never give in. Never, never, never, never." Winston Churchill

"I am always doing things I can't do; that is how I get to do them." Pablo Picasso

Repeating questions. Your niece asks a question. You repeat the question. She repeats the question. So do you. And on. "When are we going to eat?" "Well," you reply, "when *are* we going to eat?" For variety, you can tack on to the front of the question, "Oh, so you mean . . ." then repeat the question. Again and again.

Repeating words. As above. The best part comes when your niece demands that you "stop repeating my words"—which, of course, you'll instantly repeat.

Secrets. Most of the fun in a secret is in the telling. Make the universal *shoosh* sign with the finger across the lips to pique everybody's curiosity, then announce that you have a secret and swear everybody to keep it. Swear them to fiery, bloody, agonizing death if they tell. Make them *promise*. On their *lives*. On their *friends'* lives (but not their little brothers' lives. They might go for that).

> *"Hey, you want to hear a secret?"*
>
> *"Yeah!"*
>
> *"Can't tell anybody."*
>
> *"I won't."*
>
> *"Promise?"*
>
> *"I **promise**."*

> "*Okay, I'll tell you. But wait—you won't tell anybody?*"
>
> "*No. Nobody.*"
>
> "*Not even your best friends?*"
>
> "*No.*"
>
> "*Not even if they torture you?*"
>
> "*I promise.*"
>
> "*This absolutely **cannot** get out. It would ruin **everything** if they found out. **Everything**.*"
>
> "*I **promise**.*"
>
> "*Okay, okay. Here it is.*"

Take everybody away a few steps. Confess that maybe you really shouldn't tell this secret. "*Actually, you know, it's a pretty big deal. Maybe I shouldn't say it after all.*" When they howl and stamp their feet to demand that you tell, then finally, in utmost sincerity, whisper your secret.

Then say anything. It doesn't matter. Say, "*I'm going to the store to get some bread.*" Say "*Tomorrow is Wednesday.*" Say, "*Someday it might rain again.*"

"*There. Now you have the secret. Guard it with your **life**.*"

Stories. We are a story-telling species, looking for meaning and discerning patterns in everything. Kids love stories and don't really care how well crafted they are, but always give your story a structure, especially if it's long. First, the set up—what should we care about and why is it interesting to us? Second, the tension—what's happening that provides conflict or tension? Third, the resolution—how did it get fixed? Fourth, how does this relate to the protagonist, the hero or heroine?

The stories that go with things. Some things around the house have stories that kids should hear. When our niece took custody of Mom's fine mixmaster, we had to tell her about that mixer. Many years ago, Mom needed a new mixer, so was studying a mixmaster catalog. Her father, who grew up in the Depression and was a very frugal guy, asked to see what she was looking at. Mom showed Grampa the catalog, explaining that she needed a new mixer, and this was the best. Grampa was frugal, but also revered quality, and agreed that Mom should get the best. "Good quality things last longer, and that makes them cheaper," Grampa would say. He even offered to buy the mixer for Mom, a very generous gesture. Mom said, "Are you sure? It's awfully expensive." Grampa replied, "You are my only daughter. Go ahead and get the mixer." But it turns out that Grampa was looking the price for the accessory kit only, not the mixer itself. When Mom pointed out the full price tag, Grampa's face changed. It got very red and had a confused and pained look on it. After a few seconds, Grampa stammered out, "Well, I said you could get it so go ahead." Then he got very quiet, and walked around the house muttering to himself for a long time.

And that's the story of the mixmaster that my niece needs to know.

Talk like an adult. Imagine how your niece would sound if she were talking exactly like her parents. Teach her to lower her tone of voice, drop her inflection at the end of sentences, and talk about mortgage rates and comment on how nice it would be to drop in on some realtors during open house events.

One fine application of this technique is to repeat the parents' conversation as they drive along somewhere. When you repeat exactly what they said, with the same volume, tone, timbre, and inflection, this is called "backtracking." It's highly effective for driving parents crazy!

Teasers, brain. Lists of brain teasers, riddles, and puzzles are great time occupiers. Some kids call them *brain tweezers*. Here are some good ones:

Do they have the 4th of July in England? *Sure, they just don't think it's Independence Day.*

Why can't a person living in Winston-Salem, N.C. be buried west of the Mississippi River? *He could be buried there, but he might object because he's still living.*

If you had only one match and entered a room with a kerosene lamp, an oil heater, and a wood-burning stove, which would you light first? *The match.*

Some months have 30 days, some have 31; how many months have 28 days? *All 12 of them.*

A lady built a rectangular house with four sides. Each side has a southern exposure. A bear walks past the house. What color is the bear? *White. The house must be on the North Pole because all sides face south, so the bear must be a polar bear.*

Volume knob. Pretend you have a volume knob on your elbow or wrist. Turn the knob up and down and adjust the volume of your voice accordingly. You can do this with your hearing, too. "What? … Wait, lemme turn up the volume a bit. Oh, much better. What was it you were saying?"

"Why" series. Questioning is a vitally important skill for kids to develop, and it can certainly irritate their parents. The most irritating questioning strategy is the "serial why." Simple but effective. Just ask a question beginning with the word "why." Then ask "why?" again to the answer. Keep asking "why?" to answers about six times in a row. If you haven't gotten to the rock bottom of the issue, at least you've exhausted the patience of the respondent.

ZZZZ. Pretend to snore loudly. The Three Stooges ("Who are *they*?" asks your nephew) used to snore in harmony, Moe beginning with a resonant chain-saw rip, Curly joining in with a yip-yip-yip, then Larry finishing up with a nice long whistle. Make up your own snoring sequence. And if you don't know who the Three Stooges are, find out!

ANIMAL KINGDOM OF FUN

Some educators think that children learn to discriminate between objects (a higher order cognitive skill) by learning the differences between animals: wolves are different from hyenas, crocodiles from alligators, ducks from geese.

On a recent visit to a friend's house, we were goofing off in the sunroom on a rainy day when a mourning dove landed on the skylight. Three-year-old Christian was the first to notice and the last to leave. This wet bird walked around the skylight for a while, looking down and scratching around. Christian kept his finger pointed at the bird and alternated his gaze at us and then the bird. Wide-eyed, he was trying to figure out to whom he owed this great good fortune.

Animal noises. Every kid has got to be able to execute the basic animal sounds passably well and specialize in at least two. Chickens, cows, and frogs are good starter material. Cats, dogs, and sheep are a little tougher to master but obviously worth the effort. When you can a get the cat looking around the house for the intruder with your own meowing, you're getting close.

My oldest brother Marty endured a forced encampment on my apartment floor in Santa Barbara some time ago. He and Diane, his wife, their three kids, and his wife's parents couldn't find a hotel in Solvang, so they retreated to bivouac at my place. Diane's parents retired to my room, and the rest of us unfurled sleeping bags in the living room. Seconds after lights out, we heard a chicken clucking. I don't know who made this sound. (Okay, maybe it was me.) Someone else joined in with mooing sounds. A cat joined the chorus, and soon we had an active barnyard-type symphony going, punctuated by rolling belly laughs. As the symphony began to wind down, the cow or the sheep would start it all over again. Soon, Diane went to join her parents in the bedroom. I suspect she thought she was over that stage. Or maybe she just wanted some sleep.

How do you make animal noises? You use the Carnegie Hall strategy. When the Manhattan tourist asked the cab driver how to get to Carnegie Hall, the cabbie replied, "Practice, practice, practice." It's just mimicry. Listen, then imitate. Keep at it until you like the way it sounds. Or until you drive everybody out of the room. Or fool the cat.

Bugs. Insects, spiders, and other kinds of bugs are good to have around. They drive most moms crazy but don't do much harm and have great entertainment value. They're plentiful, inexpensive to obtain, there when you need them, and useful for a variety of purposes. They like to go outside, and if you put your ear right down next to them, very close, they will tell you that. They hate being squashed, so take them outside instead. Your nieces and nephews will do the same if they see you laying off the Raid.

Cooties. A gull's wing feather lay on the beach, with its late afternoon shadow arcing across the damp, tawny sand. Of course I picked it up. I had to; I was six or seven. My next-door neighbor's father was walking with us on the beach. When I picked up the feather, he said, "You better put that down. It could have cooties."

I didn't know what cooties were, but they didn't sound good and I didn't want them. I dropped that feather like it was a hot coal. But later, I thought about it. It was a feather. It was great—light but strong and curved over its 10-inch length. When I whipped it forward at arm's length, I could almost feel its lift. This feather wanted to fly. But cooties? I don't think so. Most things don't have cooties. If the item of interest isn't oozing, doesn't smell like a wolf would like to roll in it, or isn't crawling with visible life, go ahead, pick it up.

Frogs and other living things. Kids collect all kinds of small animals to investigate and bring home. Frogs are the quintessential object of attention. Smooth skinned, often green, big-eyed, they're notorious leapers. Frogs have a lot to offer. Something innate in the archaic parts of kids' brains compels them to catch small animals. Encourage them. Okay, watch out for rattlesnakes, scorpions, black widow spiders, porcupines, skunks, wasps, and komodo dragons. Most of these creatures advertise through colors, sounds, or spikes that they're packing some kind of wallop, which makes it easy to avoid them. Encourage but educate.

Kids can learn a lot by observing animals. Go with the flow and share their curiosity and excitement.

A word on how to treat these creatures. Amphibians, including frogs, toads, and salamanders, are in decline worldwide for reasons that nobody knows for sure. Habitat destruction, introduced alien species, air pollution, disease and acid rain are a few possible culprits. The combination of all of them may be intractable.

Animal Kingdom of Fun

Teach kids to respect animals and their natural habitat. Children learn to respect other people by having reverence for life. And yes, kindness to animals helps teach kindness to people, but animals are sentient beings and deserve kindness for their own sake. So show kids the proper way to care for animals. Encourage them to release wild creatures unharmed and never let them cause any animals pain or injury.

SPECIAL DAYS

Every day is a gift, we all get that. Margie's father and my father-in-law, George Washington Williams, outlived his father and his two brothers (all of whom died of heart attacks in their 40s) by 30 years. You can bet he believed that every day he woke up was a great day. None of us knows how much time we have to be around on this earth.

To a kid, every day is just another day. The sun came up yesterday and will no doubt come up tomorrow, the next day, and the day after that, and so on. Kids don't have a great appreciation for the fact that all of us are on borrowed time. A kid's day is just another day—unless you do something to make it memorable, which makes it more memorable for you, too.

April Fool's Day. What could be better? Telephone pranks, practical jokes, all kinds of teasing are on tap for this special day. Whatever the hi-jinks, make sure your nieces and nephews will think they're funny, not cruel. Funny: Call your niece and, with a disguised voice, ask,

> *"May I speak with Frank (or anybody who doesn't live there), please?"*
>
> *"You have the wrong number."*

Hang up.

Call back in a few minutes. *"I'd like to speak with Frank."*

> *"Frank doesn't live here."*

Hang up.

Call back in a few minutes. *"Please let me speak with Frank, **please**."*

> *"There's no Frank here."*

Hang up.

Call back. *"Hello, this is Frank. Has anybody called for me?"*

Other April Fool's Day pranks: Smear Vaseline on the door knobs, put a green light bulb in the refrigerator (makes the food look less than tempting), or mismatch a bunch of dad's socks in his sock drawer.

Special Days

The day *after* April Fool's is dangerous. When somebody pulls a prank on April 2nd, teach your niece or nephew to say, "April Fool's has passed, and you're the biggest fool at last." See how well *that* goes over.

Aunt and Uncle Day. Who's ever heard of this? But there *is* one—July 26. Yup, July 26, Aunt and Uncle Day. This day has competition from other obscure days of celebration packed around it. July 22 is Ratcatcher's Day. July 23 features National Hot Dog Day and Vanilla Ice Cream Day, not a bad combination. July 24 is Amelia Earhart Day. July 25 is both Culinarians Day and Threading the Needle Day. July 27 is Take Your Pants for a Walk Day. And Aunt and Uncle Day shares July 26 with All or Nothing Day. These are indisputably fine days of celebration.

On Aunt and Uncle Day, demand attention. "Where are all my *presents*? Didn't you *know*? Today is *my day*. What are you going to do for me on Aunt and Uncle Day?"

Actually, you can help here. Let's make this day a big deal. Write an op-ed piece or letter to the editor of your local paper or the *New York Times* (but not the *Washington Post* because it has no sense of humor). Post to your Facebook wall. Send out blanket email using Constant Contact. *Rent a billboard.* If we all pull together, really try, put our *backs* into it, we can make Aunt and Uncle Day at least as well known as July 31, Mutt Day.

Every day is a holiday. Ask everyone who's ever had a brush with death and that person will tell you every day is a gift. If we were smart, we'd learn from the experience of others to treat every day like a holiday. Ask the kids to create and name their own holiday. How do they want to celebrate it?

Happy Birthday song. No reason you have to reserve this song for birthdays. You can sing it any day. Every day is somebody's birthday. Sometime during dessert, just start singing the birthday song and see if you can get the kids to chime in. When it comes to the part of the song where you have to name a name, then, well, be creative.

My brother invented a style of singing the birthday song that we call Marty Style. Start out the song very softly, barely perceptible. Gradually, turn up the volume as the song progresses. By the halfway point, the group should be at half volume. By the end of the song, everyone should be screaming the words full blast. Raise the roof. This works best after you've sung the birthday song once using the proper style. Then announce, "Okay, now, *Marty Style*."

Halloween. Along with Christmas and a kid's birthday, this is his or her Big Day. Our next-door neighbor's boy asked to be a pirate last year. When his mom said she could get him a pirate costume, Aiden replied, "Not a pirate *costume*. Pirate *clothes*." This is the *real thing*.

There is something about taking on an alter ego, or avatar, or hiding behind a mask. You can be, for a few moments, whoever you choose. Of course, your niece will learn someday that this actually is real, and she can actually become whoever she wants. But for now, dressing the part, running around the neighborhood as that person (or thing), and getting rewarded with *candy*? What a deal.

Puzzles. Play h_ng m_n.

Visits from the cousins. Cousins are special. They are like brothers and sisters, but more fun. You don't see them very often. You can relate to them. You can get in minor trouble with them. You learn things from them, especially if they live in another area or go to a different school. Encourage your niece or nephew to hang out with the good ones and watch out for the ones who are trouble. You know who they are.

Weddings. A wedding day is full of promises *and* full of promise. The couple is expectant (but

I hope not expecting) and replete with visions of a wonderful life to come. Not only are the bride and groom in a buoyant mood, but so are all the spectators at the wedding. The parents, friends, siblings, business associates close enough to get invited, and other hangers-on are keyed up for a great time. Likewise your nieces and nephews. (Actually, I may have misled you. The wedding itself can be a chore; the fun begins at the reception.)

Take notice of your nieces and nephews at the wedding reception. If some were in the wedding party, say "good job." At the reception, make sure they get a chance to eat and have appropriate beverages, and most of all, *dance*. Dance with your niece. Dance with your nephew. Dance with *both* of them. At the same time.

THINGS YOU JUST MUST DO

Sometimes, kids have to act like kids. If they don't, what kind of kids would they be? The problem with this? Kid behavior is childish, and adults don't like childish behavior—especially when one of *them* is acting childish. *Childlike* is charming and wonderful; childish, not so much.

"Stop being such a child," chides a spouse. "*You*'re the one who's so childish," comes the reply. "My divorce was complicated," you might hear someone say. "There was a child involved. *My husband.*" That kind of banter. Adults don't want to be around childish behavior—in children or in adults.

Well, too bad. Here are ideas to spur your imagination about how to encourage, embellish, expand, and explode the behavior—be it childlike or childish—that your nieces and nephews need to express to be who they are. Childs.

Backwards. Doing things backwards is silly but fun. Wear clothes backwards. Talk backwards. Walk backwards. Your nieces and nephews will think you're a hero. For a few moments, they actually might not be bored.

Backyard camping. Sleeping outdoors, either under the stars or in a tent, always feels like big adventure. Camping in the woods is great, and camping in the backyard also rates as a major expedition, just without the long drive. Get everybody to agree: "Today we'll set up the tent and tonight we'll sleep in it." Organize the sleeping bags, put up the tent, find flashlights, and gather beverages and snacks. After dinner, when the sky begins to darken, head on out and crawl into the tent. Bring your flashlights, or better yet, headlamps.

On his very first camping trip, my friend Mark's nephew Craig saw the headlamps coming out and cried, "Oh great! *Adventure Helmets.*" Yes!

The more kids in the tent, the better. When somebody goes back into the house to sleep, no worry. When they all abandon the plan and head inside, no worry again. Deliver them to the house and go back into the tent. Odds are, at least one of them will stick it out with you. The next night, do it again and see if the rest don't follow. For a kid to spend even part of the night out represents a big chunk of adventure. More will ensue.

Decision tree. It's never too early to teach your nieces and nephews about decision theory and systems thinking. Thirsty? Trying to decide what to drink? Why not draw a decision tree to help?

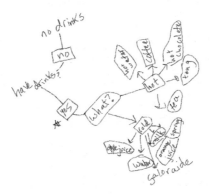

Dirt. Kids get dirty. No problem. You are the aunt or uncle, not the mother or father. You don't have to do the laundry. Let your nephew roll around in the dirt. Get grass stains on his knees. Step in the mud. Every kid will make the chance to step in a puddle. Not a bad idea. Do the same. Then teach him to wash his hands before meals. Ditto for your niece.

Discipline. This is not your department; you are not the parent. However, sometimes you might have to exert a little discipline. Your niece teases an awkward kid or does something that's mean spirited. Your nephew walks out in front of a cement truck. Do what you think is right, but follow your heart in how you do it. They grow up and they remember what you do. And worse, they will act exactly like the adults they've seen in the same situation. Set the example you wish them to follow.

"Do it again!" See **"One more time!"**

Drumming. Beating on objects to make different sounds is fun. Pretty much anything hollow works—a garbage can, a watermelon, a downed log. Percussing with your hands works, too. Percussing with sticks and clubs works better. Just don't leave dents in whatever you're wailing on.

Echoes. You can hear them in a lot more places than you'd think. Denver International Airport has an echo chamber where the trains depart for its concourses. Hint: Look at ceilings to see if they have concave surfaces. Where there's a rotunda, you'll find an echo. Pedestrian tunnels also are good candidates. Whoop it up.

Elevators. What kid doesn't want to push the elevator buttons? *All* the buttons. Remember how you jumped up when the elevator began going down? And scrunched down when it hit bottom? Your nephew and niece need to know about this.

The inside walls of the elevators in many new buildings are covered with stainless steel that was swirled with grinders. I think they look like someone got stuck in there and tried to claw his way out. Bring this to the attention of the other adults in the elevator to see if you can get a rise and then pay attention to your niece's or nephew's reactions.

Escalators. Why can't we ride on the underside of the escalator stairs? Where do those stairs go, anyway? Why does the handrail have to be black? Where is the end of that handrail, anyway? Why don't the steps in our house move? Help your niece step off the escalator at just the right time. Don't bother suggesting that she run up the down escalator. Her friends will tell her about that one when they think nobody is watching.

Fishing. A long time ago, I saw printed on a small box of fishing weights this short note: "Take a child fishing." What a great idea. It doesn't matter if you know how to fish, or even if you catch anything. Just go. Lots of things happen when you're fishing, most of which don't have anything to do with fish. Birds flit around. Insects buzz. Weather happens. And you can always talk about nothing or throw rocks into the water if boredom sets in and no other people are around to bother.

Fun anytime. There's a time and place for spontaneity, and you'll know it when you see it. For example, Pat and Lindsey and I were walking home with their kids, Helen Rose and Lillian. The hail started to come down large and hard after about three raindrops, and Helen Rose and Lillian looked scared. So we laughed. "Hail," we cried. "It's *hail*." We whooped and hollered and danced around to celebrate the hail. Helen Rose and Lillian whooped and hollered and danced, too, following our lead. All the way home.

How do you want your grandnephews to be treated? Once you decide this, you will also realize that however you and his parents treat your nephew is likely how he will one day relate to his kids. And they to theirs. So… what can you do to give your nephew a different model of behavior, an alternative way of relating to kids? The same applies to grandnieces.

Impersonations. Almost nothing is more fun than doing impersonations. Try impersonating bacon and eggs. Lie on the floor face down like a cold strip of raw bacon in a pan. Then slowly begin to pop and bubble. Flip over when one side is done. End up by thrashing about and slowly curling up on your side, as bacon wants to do. Being an egg is good, too. Crouch. Slap your thigh loudly and spring to the floor. Thrash about until that side is done, then turn (if you like your eggs over). Throw out an impersonation challenge like this to your nieces and nephews.

Invisible. Pretend to be invisible in key situations. In crowded places such as shopping centers and the like, sure. But also at family events or any everyday situation. Explain to your nephew that even if it seems people are looking at him, they're actually looking *through* him at something else. They don't really see him, so he should just go about the business of being invisible and not worry about anyone else. If somebody speaks to him, maybe he can answer as a disembodied voice. Or no answer at all. Who talks to invisible people, anyway?

Invite them to help. See **Helping in the kitchen** and apply it to any situation.

Kicking rocks off a trail. You're walking down a trail or sidewalk with your nephew or niece. Twenty feet ahead, you spy a rock or pinecone in the way. Say, "Watch *this*." Measure your stride so that one instep lands exactly next to the rock. Then flick your foot to the inside, deftly flicking the rock off the path.

After that, you can race your nephew or niece to the next obstacle to be flicked away.

Knots. In the day of Velcro shoes, minicarabiners, and bungee cords, tying knots is becoming a lost art. But every kid does need to know how to tie a shoe knot (take one extra turn before tucking in the last loop for a bomb-proof shoe knot). And a square knot, in case they have to reef a sail unexpectedly. And the bowline, because it's the king of knots and every kid should be comfortable with the king. Better yet, give a knot board for a present. Knot boards are boards with the names and pictures of the knots printed on them, with two attached pieces of rope for practice. A life lesson.

Laughter. Psychologist Fritz Perls said that fear is excitement without breathing. It's impossible to hold your breath while laughing. So, when the chips are down and everyone is gripped in fear, laugh. Loudly. Get everybody around you laughing. As you get them breathing and laughing, the fear turns to excitement and the world seems "right" again. The next two related entries merely tickle the surface of the laughter category.

"Hysterical laughter leads to crying." Our father often made this observation. Once kids get whipped up to a certain frenzy level, the hysterical laughter begins, and someone will be crying soon, 100 percent guaranteed. If you can't calm down the mod, go get the Kleenex.

Laughing for no reason. Whenever you can, just laugh out loud. When your nephew or niece asks, "What?" just say, "Oh, nothing." Everybody knows that people are more creative and more productive when in a humorous mood. So laugh. Why not?

Lists. Being natural collectors, kids like to make lists. It's just collecting ideas on paper instead of rocks or shells in a box. Make a list with your niece of everything you plan to do for the next 20 minutes. Make up a grocery list, then take her shopping. Be inclusive:

Grocery List

1. Decide what we are going to eat.

2. Check cupboards and refrigerator for what we need.

3. Find car keys.

4. Select route.

5. Open the front door.

6. Exit the house.

7. Close the front door.

8. Walk to the car.

9. Find the car keys in pocket.

10. Insert keys into car door lock (or squirt that chirping sound at the car to force the locks to open, if you have that kind of equipment).

11. Open car door.

12. Get in.

13. Close car door.

14-456. Continue along this same line.

"Living room is not a playground." This is closely related to "Hysterical laughter leads to crying." Only this time, it was our mother who said it. Once the wrestling starts, it's going to be a lot of fun until somebody gets squashed or nicks the corner of the coffee table. Unlike in the movies, people rarely die from this, so it's okay. The parents will appreciate it if you take the wrestling to the Wrestling Room, or a close equivalent. Not that we care overly much to cater to the parents.

Manners. Manners are good for kids to acquire, and you are in a strong position to lead by example. The parents will harp on this, and your voice will drown in that same sea if you merely parrot them. But by *demonstrating* good manners, your influence will be powerful. Dramatically whip the napkin from the table, wave it like a surrender around your head, and then plop it in your lap. Voila, you are leading by example.

Mean things. Don't do them, and don't let your nieces and nephews get away with doing them. There's plenty of that out there already and we need to have less. When you see something mean going on, just say in a firm but matter of fact voice, "You know, we just don't do that around here."

Mr. Literal. Do everything your nephew says exactly as he says it.

"I'd like some water," says your nephew.

"I'm sure you would," you reply.

"Okay, can I have some water?"

"Sure, why not?"

*"**May** I have some water?"*

"You may, my friend, you may," you assure him.

*"I **want** water."*

"Yes, you mentioned that."

*"Will you **please** get me some water?"* he asks, in his most polite voice.

"Yes."

"But you aren't getting it."

"Oh, you mean now? Okay, let me get you some." But as you get up to go fetch it: *"What kind of water do you want?"* Uh oh, another round of Mr. Literal is coming.

Naps. They're good when you're tired. They're best when spontaneous. Planned naps in no way compare to just falling asleep. Twenty minutes is a good duration. Longer than that and beware. The kids will be groggy for hours.

Nice things for no reason. Lots of people repay favors. Some people don't have to wait for something good to happen to return the favor; they just do nice things for no reason. You may have heard the famous ones, such as paying the bridge toll for the car behind you. You could have some fun with your siblings' kids by saying, "Let's pick up that piece of litter and toss it in the bin, just for no reason." They may look at you strangely at first, but they'll soon get on board. If someone is struggling with grocery bags in the market, offer to lift a bag. But be careful. Once I tried to help an elderly lady drag her luggage through the revolving door in a Baltimore hotel. She questioned sharply, "Do you work here?" "No," I said. She yanked those bags back as though I were a thief. Maybe I need to dress better.

No seriousness. Call it a rule. With a very stern presence, announce, "For the next twenty minutes, there will be *no seriousness* around here." Set the countdown timer. Enforce the rule. If your niece or nephew does something non-silly, call out "*No seriousness*." Then hang a spoon on your face.

Noise mimicking. The world is full of different sounds. Motorized equipment, clanging cook pans, ringing bowls and glasses. When you hear a sound you like, repeat it a few times. Entice your nephew to join in and mimic that sound. A bunch of times. The bus honks, so we honk. Loudly.

Noise versus quiet. There's a time for quiet, but mostly, noise is better. Raucous noise is best, especially at inconvenient times. Quiet has its time, too, especially when it's *dis*quieting. But noise is a fine thing.

A leader in an adults-only community in the Sierra Nevada foothills in California fought hard against a mixed-use housing development proposed for next door. "Our community isn't ready for the noise those children would make," she complained. Imagine the sounds of children laughing and playing and making noise. How dreadful. Somebody should have invoked the *No seriousness* rule on that lady.

On the other hand, sometimes it's just too quiet. Investigate. Somebody is up to something.

Older kids. Older kids know stuff, they can do stuff, and they will do stuff that younger kids can't, and that attracts the younger kids' curiosity in a big way. Some older kids communicate well with your nieces and nephews. They help them learn, set a good example, model the behaviors you hope your nephew or niece will adopt. Other older kids can be trouble. When your nieces and nephews suddenly take notice and say in soft tones, "Uh-oh, *big kids*," pay attention. Learn to tell the one type of older kid from the other. Discourage interaction with those whose behavior you wouldn't want to see mimicked by your nephew or niece.

"One more time!" See **"Do it again!"** The main point here is that, if everything is working, your niece or nephew will not want to quit and will beg to keep going. Oblige. You toss your nephew across the swimming pool all afternoon. Your arms are shot. Your back complains. Your fingers are like prunes. But all you hear, when he surfaces and dog paddles back to you for the 451st time, is, "Again!" Well, okay. You hope for a thunderstorm that will close the pool soon, and you toss him again.

Point out inconsistencies in parents' behavior. Often, parents give instructions to their children that they themselves don't follow. Help your niece or nephew point out these discrepancies. "Dad, you said never to use the word 'hate,' but you just said you 'hate' doing your taxes. Why is that?"

Pretending. Always a winner, you can pretend lots of things to evoke good humor. Pretending to be a robot, for example, has gotten a lot easier with the advent of roller-shoes and MP3 player earplugs. You can also pretend to step in gross things, play dead, wash clean dishes with no water. When you see a pile of dog doo on the sidewalk, pretend not to see it and step your heel four inches away, then quickly turn your toe to the side at the last second to miss the pile. Practice this ahead of time. A misstep is no good here.

Reading. Will Rogers once said, "Man learns best by doing two things. One is by reading and the other is by association with smarter people." *You* are among the "smarter people" Will is referring to. As an influential person to your niece and nephew, perhaps the best thing you can do is to model an infectious love for reading. Let them catch you reading, talk about what you're reading, and best of all, read to them. Even short snippets. That's smart!

Really scary moments. When really scary things happen, scream. Something falls to the kitchen floor. Scream. A door slams. Scream. Your brother walks into the room. Scream. Loud. Twice. At least. Okay, the thing doesn't even have to be that scary. Scream anyway.

Routine things. Show joy in performing routine duties with style, purpose, and intention. What's become rote for you may still be novel to your niece and nephew, just as it once was for you. Go back and wash the dishes, water the plants, sort the mail, and take out the trash as though it were your first time. Explain how fun it is to be able to do these daily chores. "Man, I *love* doing these dishes. When they are done and put away, you know your job is finished. That's a great feeling."

Scaring. Kids love a good scare; don't ask me why, but they do. Hide in a broom closet. Spring from behind a curtain. Jump out from behind a bush.

Things You Just Must Do

How you set this up is key. You might say, "Do you know where the broom is? I can't find it anywhere. I'll give a quarter to anyone who can find the broom first." Then duck in the, yes indeedy, broom closet. After the setup, the scream is the next most important action. While raising your hands, palms down, wrists slightly bent, just above the level of your shoulders a la the boogie man, let out a big scream!

Silence. Not golden, but more rare than gold with kids around, silence provides the counterpoint to all that noise—hence its value. You can't honestly appreciate the noise until it's gone. Most likely, you'll have to gain a few seconds of silence by challenging your nieces and nephews to a contest. You'd say, "I'll bet you can't keep quiet for sixty seconds." Or you'd challenge them to "notice how many different sounds you can hear in the next one minute." That's guaranteed to work for about 44 seconds.

Singing. Singing is fun. At Uncle Matt's wedding, one of the three year olds burst out into the birthday song just as best man Gavin was trying to settle the throng to offer the toast. It must have seemed to Gavin like the thing to do, so he, holding his champagne glass on stage, just went with it and helped him lead the singing. After all, somebody in the room, or somebody *somewhere*, was probably having a birthday. Why not?

Skipping. Most kids know how to skip, and they do it spontaneously and without consciousness. Wouldn't they be surprised to see *you* skipping? Do it just once and they'll wonder if they really saw it. Skip enough to catch their attention, and they will ask you why you're skipping. You reply, "Who's skipping?" That should confuse them—for a minute anyway.

Sneezing. A loud, hearty sneeze is wonderful. Hold it in daintily at your own peril. Better to let it out, project it, and watch your nephew's and niece's reactions. Of course, use a hanky. It's possible to pronounce some words during a sneeze, but it's not easy. Try *"Shazaaammm!"* or *"Sasparilla!"* for starters, and build on that.

Spontaneity. Part of the oft-cited but not truly appreciated "childlike wonder" is a kid's immediacy of attention. You see, this immediacy is unappreciated because it's frequently quite inconvenient. "Let's go outside," says two-year-old Max, who in four minutes wants to go back inside, which lasts for five minutes before he declares that he wants to go outside. Max exhibits childlike wonder, focusing on what's within his grasp and vision. He's being spontaneous. He's being a kid.

Things You Just Must Do

Go with it. The skill of matching the spontaneity of a two-year-old child is innate in all aunts and uncles, but dingy and gray, cobwebbed and shriveled from a society that values convenience over all. Reawaken this skill. Say yes. Go with Max. He'll show you what to do.

Staring. Polite manners prevent staring at strangers, but no such rule applies to having stare-downs with your siblings' kids. Set up a contest and use a timer because they will want to measure their progress in ensuing stare-down rounds.

Superstitions. Superstitious beliefs came from somewhere, and we shouldn't quibble about their being unscientific, old-fashioned, and archaic. For example, why not put your shoes on a table? Well, it's rather unsanitary for one thing, but is it dangerous? Throw salt over your shoulder when somebody puts shoes on a table. Why salt? I don't know that, either. And never give a knife as a present because giving a knife cuts the friendship. So you have to sell the knife; get a nickel for it. Or not, but who wants the risk?

Surprises. The best! Spring them often for the most trivial or important occasions. Be sure to announce them with great fanfare.

Swinging on gates. It's a small thing that not many people in urban areas get to do. But if you and your niece or nephew ever come across a gate on a rural road, by all means, swing on it. Just once. Then run because the gate owner won't like it—that is, unless he harkens back to being young and swinging on gates, too.

Upside-down drinking. Sometimes the only way to get rid of hiccups (after trying scaring, of course) is to get a glass of water, bend at the waist, and try drinking from the glass while your head is upside down. You don't even need to have hiccups to try this!

Walking funny. Consider these possibilities:

> *Trucking* using the same arm and leg going forward together instead of opposite arms and legs
>
> *Trotting* with a quick cadence, tiny steps, and little patting motions with your hands
>
> *Synching* your gait with your nephew's or niece's, then periodically giving a quick hop to go out of phase
>
> *Walking like a gorilla* and add sound effects for high-definition impact.

Things You Just Must Do

Water. Loren Eisley said, "If there is magic on this planet, it is contained in water." Puddles, hoses, aquaria, creeks, ponds, lakes, ocean beaches. Tubs and sinks, buckets, pitchers, glasses. Ripples on a pond, sunlight sparkles. Waves. Wetness. Cold water. Warm water. Salty water. Green pond water. Ice. Slush. Snow. Faucets. Water striders. Dragonflies. Turtles. Guppies. Algae. Splashing. Skipping rocks. Sailing leaves and sticks on the current. Cooling the feet. Blowing bubbles underwater. Swimming, wading, racing the waves. Making a raft. Making a mess. Toweling off. Air drying. Drinking water.

Whistling. Ah, whistling, an important life skill. Learning to whistle takes time, patience, and stick-to-it-iveness. Be prepared to help your niece or nephew stick with it. Demonstrate, offer encouragement, and just be there. "Tune" whistling is different from "getting-somebody's-attention" whistling. Teach them both.

Worm song. If your nieces and nephews don't already know this song, they should. Sing it loudly and gravelly, with emphasis on the last word. It's sung to the tune of, well, the worm song.

> *Nobody likes me*
>
> *Everybody hates me*
>
> *Think I'm gonna eat some worms.*

Short, fat, juicy ones.

Long slim slimy ones.

Itsy bitsy fuzzy wuzzy WORMS.

Repeat, *ad nauseum.*

Yawns. Think for a second about a big, gaping yawn. Place yourself in a time when you saw somebody yawn—a huge one, with lots of weird sounds. Are you yawning now? Do you feel a yawn coming on?

It's fun to make somebody else yawn, especially in a group. Chain reactions are the best, like doing The Wave at a baseball game. Can you keep the yawn going around in a circle? Hey, cover your mouth.

Inducing yawns are fun and ruining yawns can have their place, too. Simple. When you induce a yawn in your nephew, just lightly stick your finger in his mouth without touching anything. Yawn interrupted. Just like that.

Yelling. Whenever you're in a tunnel or similar echo-chamber, start yelling and get everybody to yell with you. Go high, go low, harmonize. Whoop. Yodel. Ululate. Show off your best uvula. You don't need a reason.

JUST HANGING OUT

Most kids have not yet been infected by the hurry sickness. They don't have punch lists, project plans, and scheduling software. They know how to sit around and not fret to the point of producing stress-related diseases. They only know how to hang out.

But hanging out isn't all that wonderful after the lack of stimulation sets in, often in about 12 minutes. "What do you want to do?" "I dunno. What do *you* want to do?" When you get to that point, you have to *work* at hanging out. You need things to do that aren't really activities, just different ways of doing, well, nothing. Here are some. You can think of more.

Band-Aids. For who knows what reason, kids hone in on cuts. They like to show you their cuts and scrapes and really get fascinated with yours—the gorier the better. If they can't have a cut or scrape, they can still have a band-aid. A good supply of band-aids is solid entertainment. Help the kids plaster themselves, then go show Mom, who just might pass out from shock at the sight.

Bathroom humor. At a certain age, kids figure this out on their own. You don't need to encourage it. And once they start, you don't have to egg them on.

The Belt. Sometimes, at least in times past, children needed more discipline, which was administered with The Belt. My siblings and I grew up terrified of The Belt, although none of us ever felt it. Dad would ask, very calmly, whether we needed The Belt. No, we didn't, thanks. A little less obstreperous behavior followed.

Just Hanging Out

The Belt really existed. Dad told us it was a firefighter's belt. It was white canvas, about six inches wide, rough, very thick, with two rows of holes and two of those thingies on belt buckles that you stick into the hole in the belt. The buckle made of massive metal must have weighed a pound and would have killed Godzilla with one blow. Some belt. It hung on the garage wall from a nail driven above the folded ping-pong table The Belt never came down, but we didn't doubt that it might be put into action at any time.

Belts. Here's a neat thing kids need to know about belts: You can double them up and snap the two halves together to make a loud popping sound, which is great fun. Try it often and get good at it because sometime somewhere you will need to show kids how to do this.

Books. Books are wonderful. I like the way they feel, how the pages sound when you fan them, how the paper smells, their whole physical presence. And I really like to read. Kids often want to sit with you while you read to see what on earth you're doing.

I read aloud to kids sometimes, but I've learned that the subject matter is key in maintaining their attention. On a backpack trip one summer, I brought along a book on adult learning, juicy summer reading for certain. During a thundershower, I retreated with Cate and her kids John and Kelly to the tent where I began to read aloud from a chapter of this riveting book. John and Kelly clapped their hands over their ears and made howling noises to get me to stop. And I did stop, but only until they came up for air, so I could start up again. I'm sure they loved it, and I fully expect both of them to become adult educators when they grow up.

Treating books well is important. There's wide latitude in what "well" means here. Obvious trashing is recognizable and verboten, but see **Cartoons** as an example of nontraditional book treatment.

Brothers and sisters. They're precious. They're a pain. The older ones are like gods. The younger ones are like stickers in your socks. And they all grow up. And get big. Some bigger than you. And they remember things. Your nephews and nieces don't know this yet, but you can help. A little gentle instruction when you see them being mean to each other—plus encouragement when you catch them being wonderful—will save them severe thumpings when their little brothers aren't so little anymore. They revere you. It will stick.

Cleaning up. Just to prove that anything can be fun with the right frame of mind, make a game of cleaning up. Honest, this can work. Set a time limit for polishing windows, create competition between kids for the cleanest bathroom, express joy and enthusiasm for cleaning the kitchen. Unless you are Tom Sawyer, you will have to be part of the competition. Good luck.

Capturing the moment. To a kid whose focus is immediate and all-consuming, every moment is full on and in High Definition. Whatever you're in the middle of, it might be easier to go with the instant shift in attention that your niece or nephew flitters to. So just say yes. When your niece does a 180-degree shift in attention from rearranging your DVD collection to chasing the cat around the living room, go with it. See if you can recapture the nimbleness of the spontaneous focus you, too, used to have.

Cartoons. The ones on TV, fine. The ones you make with your sister's kids, better. Draw a picture of people or things in action, then fill in the dialog bubble. Who cares if you can't draw? The fun is in the doing and the doodling, not in its perfection.

Try this: Take an old paperback book and use each page to create a cartoon movie. Draw something on each page in a slightly different position. When you flip the pages, you view the movie. One book shows a movie of a locomotive crashing into a wall with a spot that looks like a tunnel painted on it. How artistic.

Collecting things. Kids are born collectors. They don't care what they collect—rocks, flowers, whatever. Our next-door neighbor Aiden has a toy metal detector. He has collected full five-gallon buckets of bent, rusty nails, assorted nuts and bolts, and an occasional railroad spike! It doesn't matter what the kids want to collect, but you will know because they'll start picking up stuff. They'll probably ask you to hold it when the items overfill their pockets and hands. Get another bucket. Help find stuff. Go with it.

Crying. It happens. Cry along with your niece and nephew. Ham it up. Outcry them, dramatically, loudly, ridiculously. Watch tears turn to laughter. Physiologically, kids (and adults, too) can't cry when they're laughing.

Cuts and bruises. If you have any cuts on your hands or somewhere else, your niece or nephew will notice them and want to look them over. I don't understand the morbid fascination kids have with cuts and bruises, but they have it. They're not only captivated by other people's cuts, but also by their own. And they love to put band-aids on those cuts, no matter how minor. (See **Band-Aids**.) Keep a supply of band-aids on hand. Use them liberally.

Grossness. Gross is engrossing. Nasal crust, flatulence, road kill, drain slime; these are all fascinating things. Disgust is a lifesaving human behavior. Kids have an instinct to check out gross things, like the internal organs of squashed frogs, rotting pond vegetation and anything with maggots. They do have this instinct for fascination, and also an instinct to look at it but *don't let them eat it*. Once they get to be nine months old, anyway. You, too, can pretend to be fascinated with pond scum.

Handshakes. Every kid needs to know how to negotiate a proper handshake. Grab the hand straight up and down (none of this weird dominant power game twist-the-wrist stuff), look the person right in the eye, and say, "Hello." Squeeze firmly but don't show your strength. Then let go. That's the traditional way.

But there's more.

> *The lumberjack handshake:* Grab a-hold then saw back and forth as though using a crosscut.
>
> *The fisherman's handshake:* Grab a-hold and pull in the other's hand.

The electrician's handshake. Shocking. Buzz and jump around like you have your toe in a light socket.

The dairy farmer's handshake: It's udderly up to you to figure this one out.

Hitting and kicking. Prevent it. Explain that this kind of behavior is not okay. Say, "We just don't do that kind of thing around here."

Ideas. Announce, "Hey, I have an idea," as a way to place special emphasis on whatever you are about to say. It doesn't matter if the idea needs emphasizing or not. It makes your words special whether they are or aren't.

Jokes. This is a core skill for a kid, both on the telling side and the "getting it" side. Many jokes aren't funny, but almost everybody laughs anyway to disguise the fact that they don't think it's funny and therefore probably didn't get it. After all, they don't want others to think they're not very smart.

The great thing about kids—and in my estimation the real reason that people even *have* kids—is that trite, hackneyed, worn-out-a-thousand-times-over jokes still get their reactions. The cornier the better.

"Do you know how many people are dead in that cemetery?"

"No, how many?"

"All of them."

See?

Knock-knock jokes are great fun. "Knock knock. Who's there? Frankfurter. Frankfurter who? Frankfurter lovely evening." Okay, so this joke was invented before kerosene lamps and isn't funny when you read it. Well, it isn't very funny when you hear it either, unless you are six years old and have never heard it before. In this case, it's an absolute scream.

Puns also rate highly, especially when kids haven't yet learned that the proper response to a pun is a groan. This makes them a great audience because nobody likes a groaner.

"Got a match?"

"Not since Superman died."

"What's brown and sticky?"

"A stick."

"How do you get down from an elephant?"

"You don't. You get down from a duck."

"What's this:

brown

---

coat"

"Brown overcoat."

"What's this:

wear

---

long"

"No, it's long under wear."

Make a circle with your thumb and forefinger and say, "Can you poke your head through this?" Then put that hand against your forehead and poke your other index finger through to poke your head. A no-brainer.

Humor. Humor is actually a sophisticated skill (one I haven't mastered yet but I love trying!) and indicates that kids are thinking. They find humor in others' jokes long before they can deliver them (on purpose) themselves.

When a kid tells his or her first few knock-knock jokes, they probably won't make much sense or be very funny, but aunts and uncles should laugh anyway. For instance, "Knock knock." "Who's there?" "A cow." Then peals of laughter. Yup, that's the whole joke. Well, a cow at the door *is* funny. Actually, that one's not so bad.

Jumping on the furniture. We really shouldn't. But if it's their parents' furniture, well, why not?

TOYS, TRICKS, AND TRIAL BALLOONS

Toys are bought. Toys are built. Toys are invented from junk and household items and nothing special. Some toys and props, like crazy glasses, must be purchased. But you can make most toys by taking ordinary things and just using them like toys. Bottles, coins, anything you can press into service when you need them. Read on!

Bottles. You can do heroic things with bottles, and kids need to know how that works! Blow into an empty bottle to make the sound of a ship's whistle. Look at the sky through the bottom of an (empty) bottle. Hang an empty bottle from your upper lip by sucking the air out of it and then gently moving the inside of your lip over the opening.

Bubbles. Bubbles float, glisten, shimmer with rainbows—and they pop. You don't need fancy stuff to make them, but they're always a hit. Saliva bubbles are easy to make; the material is readily available and cheap. They take practice, but they're worth it. Soap bubbles, while requiring more gear, have their advantages. A few weeks ago, I got hold of bubbles at a wedding I attended with a friend and her two kids. On the drive from the wedding ceremony to the reception, it seemed to be the thing to do to roll down the car window and let the 35-miles-per-hour wind speed blow bubbles all over the car interior. It's unbelievable how many bubbles you can fit into a car before the driver gets extremely annoyed.

Bubble wrap is a special class of bubble. Soap and saliva bubbles are silent when they pop, but bubble wrap provides extra excitement. I've heard that if you pop all the bubbles in a sheet of bubble wrap, it will set you free. I must be free many times over but I don't know what's supposed to happen to me now. Walking on bubble wrap is a good way to pop the bubbles. Strategically placing bubble wrap on the floor in high-traffic areas of the home can be highly entertaining.

Camera (invisible). Click. What did you get? Free and readily available, the invisible camera is a perennial favorite. Pretend you have a camera. Still or video or both. Hand it to your niece and ask her to take some photos. Of anything. Then ask her what she got. Color or black and white? Still or movie?

Big or small? What's in the picture? Next step: have her show her invisible pictures from the invisible camera to a person in the photo.

Cereal-box fort. More fun at breakfast. Simply make a wall between you and the kids with a couple of cereal boxes. Then hide behind the wall and peer over the top or between the boxes once in a while. This gets kids' attention. Not as much as the sound of a quarter hitting the sidewalk or the rattle of a rattlesnake, but enough. When they start to get annoyed with you giving them the eyeball, then quit doing it, keep it going longer, or get out of Dodge.

Chocolates. What's in those filled chocolates that show up in slim, white boxes during the holiday season? Unless you work at See's Candies or have a secret decoder ring for the swirl pattern on top, you never know—until it's too late. Only when you've bitten into the chocolate and hold it away from your mouth to look at it can you identify the filling. And only then do you know whether you like it better than—or not as much as—what you'd hoped would be inside. Until you've used intrusive analysis, such as biting a hole in the top, you can never be sure if the filling will be really tasty or really gross.

But there *is* a simple sample technique every kid needs to know: *bite a hole in the bottom*! If you like the insides, chomp it on down. If you don't like it (Eeewww! Weird white creamy stuff!), then replace the chocolate in the little crinkly brown paper cup, reinsert into the box, and try another. Nobody will know that sampling happened, and what parents don't know can't hurt them.

Clear contact paper. Pick up a roll when you're at the store. You can do all kinds of activities with clear contact paper. Here goes.

> *Make a book.* Have your niece or nephew design a front cover and a back cover, staple in a couple of pages inside, and then cover the outside with clear contact paper (CCP).
>
> *Arrange leaves and flowers* on a piece of cardboard and cover with CCP to make a permanent specimen.
>
> *Make any kind of art* and cover it for posterity.
>
> *Make outdoor signs* ("Take your dog to your own yard" or "No Depleted Uranium Allowed") and weatherproof them with clear contact paper for posting in the yard.

Clothes and getting dirty. They're kids. They're active. They get into things. They *need* to get into things. As long as they aren't getting into danger, they're just doing what they need to do. Sometimes, if things go right, they will get dirty. And they'll get their clothes dirty—unless their parents rant and rave about the laundry, which will inhibit their innate curiosity. This curiosity should be celebrated and rewarded, not beat down. So, simply observe the dirt and compliment them. "Hey, nice grass stains. Where'd you get those?" It's easy for aunts and uncles to do this because it's the parents, not they, who have to do the laundry.

Coins. Sometimes kids do something good. You can reinforce their positive actions by spreading around a little cash. *"Hey, thanks for helping out with dinner. Here's a quarter."* Okay, the parents are getting riled and saying, "But they should be helping with dinner and we don't want them thinking they have to get paid for doing what they ought to do anyway." Whatever. Positive reinforcement is a more powerful shaper of behavior than anything (certainly more than ignoring the kid), so give them a little positive reinforcement. Coinage. Try with pennies, but older kids might shake their heads and say, *"Uh uh. Silver money."*

"You mean dimes and nickels?"

*"Uh huh. And **quarters**."*

Now they're also learning math and negotiation skills.

Cones. Those giant orange highway construction cones make great megaphones. Next time you're walking down the street with your niece and nephew and you see an orange cone, let them walk by, then pick up the cone and, megaphone style, loudly shout, *"Everybody out of the pool"* or something equally outrageous.

Crazy glasses. Find them at toy stores—clear plastic straws bent into the shape of eyeglass frames. Drink colorful drinks through them and watch the liquid swirl through the straws.

"Go to" in books. In one of the kid's books that isn't expensive, write "Go to page 24" in the top margin. On page 24 write, "Go to page 36." On page 36, write another page, then more and more. Finally, write in the margin, "Go to page 24." Drives 'em crazy.

Hanger gong. Wire clothes hangers make fine gongs. Hang one from another and use a third to strike. Stunning.

Handkerchiefs. Dramatic, theatrical nose blowing is a fine art that nieces and nephews need to master. Imitation is the quickest way to mastery. Set a good example.

How many things can you do with a (paper cup)? Contests are good and most kids love a challenge. Cast the gauntlet with a paper cup or a piece of string, a paper clip, a rubber band. Set a time, pay attention to the clock, and announce the remaining time dramatically. While the clock is ticking, count the number of things they do with the object.

Hundred dollar bill. If you come across one, save it in your wallet to flash it around to your nieces and nephews. For whatever reason, they'll remember forever that you're the kind of person, a smooth and amazing enough person, that you carry around Benjamins.

Light is good. The phrase "Let there be light" started it all. John Muir called the Sierra Nevada mountains the "Range of Light." Stevie Wonder said, "You are the sunshine of my life." And sunshine is, after all, light. You can find plenty of fun things to do with light. Here are a few ideas.

Flashlight through the head and more. Put a switched-on light against one ear and hold up your hand about five inches from your other ear, palm facing your ear. Ask your niece or nephew if the light is coming through.

How about the flashlight-in-the-mouth trick? In the dark, place the flashlight in your mouth to have your cheeks light up. Press the flashlight to the palm of your hand and see how weirdly red the light comes through. Best of all, shine the light up from below your chin to make your face to look scary at night. If you don't believe me, check this out in a mirror.

Pouring light. Given the nature of water and the properties of light, you can pour light like water. Stick a turned-on waterproof flashlight in a pitcher of water and pour the water into a glass. Put some red food coloring in the water and make liquid rubies.

Magic Bic pen. Take a standard, clear-barreled Bic pen, remove the top, and then moisten your thumb and index finger. When you're ready, dramatically announce, "This is a magic pen." Line up the cap with the point of the pen and squeeze intently until the cap magically jumps toward the point.

Microphone (imaginary). Related to the imaginary camera, the imaginary microphone is great fun. Conduct interviews about major and trivial events. Imitate sportscasters. For added yucks, pretend the microphone is hooked up to a tape recorder and play back what your niece or nephew just said.

Mole doorbells. If you have a mole on your head or arm or hand, a younger niece or nephew will soon say, "What's *that* thing?" You reply, "Why, it's a *doorbell*. Push it." When she pushes it, make a doorbell sound. If you have more than one mole, you have to have different doorbell rings ready when she or he presses each one. Just don't get the noises mixed up.

Money (value of). Kids don't bother to pick up pennies anymore. Point this out next time your nephew and niece pass up a penny. You say,

> *"Hey, there's a penny; let's pick it up."*
>
> *"Aw, it's just a penny."*
>
> *"There are children in China who are starving and would be overjoyed to eat that penny."*

Keep up this banter as long as you can. Consider it positive feedback when they begin to roll their eyes.

Plants. A lot of plants are good fun to play with.

Bedstraw (genus *Galium*) has Velcro-like hooks that cling to most clothes when you toss a piece of the plant at your niece or nephew.

Maple seeds make great rhinoceros horns. Take a maple seed and tear it in half between the two wings. Discard the part with the stem. Peel apart the thick portion along the line separating the two parts of the seed end. A Post-It note-quality glue in the seed lets you stick the seed to your nose or chin or cheek or forehead. Very attractive.

Filaree (also called cranesbill, genus *Erodium*) has a long, needle-like seed that works to make scissors. Here's how. With your thumbnail, slit one of the long parts of the seed. Insert a second seed into the slit, and you have scissors. With a mature seed, hold it in the palm of your hand and gently blow on it. The tail of the seed will coil up, and the seed itself will try to drill itself into your palm (which is how the seed plants itself into the soil in wet weather).

Rocks. Many parts of the country have lots of rocks. Even places that don't have rocks have rocks. New Orleans doesn't have rocks because thousands of feet of sediments from the Mississippi River have covered them. But even southern Louisiana has rocks brought in as beds for road building. That's one place where you and your nephew can explore and find them.

Fort Worth, Texas, has rocks, too. In a ravine near Margie's father's house near Fort Worth, our 7-year-old nephew Riley and his father Robert took us to look for them. And we found something better than rocks; we found fossils. We found fossilized scallop shells and clamshells from when Texas was an ocean. We even found fossils as big as Riley's hand with his fingers spread wide. Wise young Riley put it all in perspective when he said, "This is like finding gold rubies."

Rubber bands and other projectiles. The lawyers would want me to preface this with warnings to wear eye protection, body armor, shin guards, welder's helmets, and massive yellow jackets favored by firefighters before talking about shooting rubber bands. But search as hard as you like, you'll find no mention of body armor in this book.

Singing glasses. Did you know that drinking glasses with a base and a stem can learn to sing? Hold the base with a few fingers (avoid touching the stem), wet the index finger of your free hand, and run it around the rim of the glass until the glass begins to sing. You will have created beautiful sounds. This topic will be closely related to "Spills" if you are careless about it.

Spoons. A versatile implement, the spoon. Make music by nesting two together with your finger inserted between the stems and percuss away. Or try hanging a spoon from your nose or even your cheek if you have the right physiognomy. You might have to fog the bowl of the spoon with your breath to get the friction you need.

Static shocks. Static electricity is wonderful. Free, easily accessible with the right kind of carpet and weather, static shocks can be fun. Shuffle your feet across the carpet on a dry, cold day, and then find your niece's or nephew's earlobe to brush with your fingertip. *Zap!* You've made electricity!

Sticking balloons. Balloons work well with static electricity. Blow up a balloon and rub it on your pile or wool sweater gingerly. Then bet your nephew or niece that you can make the balloon stick to the wall without glue or tape. Static charge between the wall and the balloon will do the rest. Stick it to the wall and collect your winnings.

Tape recorder (imaginary). Aligned with the imaginary camera and imaginary microphone, this item is indispensable for "taping" what people say— for both posterity and instant replay.

Tattoos. Temporary tattoos and face painting are terrific good fun. Street fairs and events nowadays have face painters around, and you can get temporary tattoos at toy stores and even some of those gumball-type vending machines. The emphasis on tattoos is *temporary*.

Time capsule. Decide to get everybody together and make a time capsule. Assemble a tube with screw-down ends and have each person find objects that represent the current time in history. Insert the collected items into the tube, write and date a note, stuff it in the tube, and then seal it and bury it in the backyard.

Nowadays, companies make real, honest-to-goodness time capsules. But it's not necessary to buy anything. An empty jelly jar works, too.

Toaster-thermometer trick. Take an oral thermometer. Hold it over a warm toaster for a few moments until the thermometer registers about 108 degrees F., and then have your niece or nephew run to Mommy saying, "I think I have a temperature." Show Mom the mercury. "Just kidding, Sis."

Toy store. Next time you're in a toy store, fill your pockets with inexpensive toys of all kinds. You don't know when you'll need them. Pay for them before you leave the store.

Upside-down glasses. Wear your eyeglasses upside down. Or make eyeglasses out of your hands and wear them, too.

Whistles. A whistle makes a fine gift for your nieces and nephews. Good coaches' whistles are still made of shiny metal and plastic whistles of all colors are plenty serviceable. Wooden whistles carved in the shape of a locomotive and sounding like a train are classy. Hint: If you give one niece or nephew a whistle, give all of them a whistle. Then leave before the parents find out.

Windows. Windows are amazing. They keep air out but let light in. They're also a great medium for artistic expression. Windows take grease pencil, water-based markers, and soap for writing and drawing. Both bar soap and shaving cream make it easy to draw pictures on the windows. As long as you don't use anything scratchy and make sure kids leave the walls alone, you're safe.

Water vapor is my favorite artistic medium on glass. Windows that fog up from the inside in wet weather are a genuine bonanza, one of life's great pleasures. An ideal drawing medium, the vapor on windows works great for tic-tac-toe, hangman, and other games that have become too routine for paper.

For a special treat, teach your siblings' kids the proper way to look out of frosted windows. Don't just smear the droplets around with your hand; that's crude and reveals a lack of style and imagination. With the tip of your index finger, carefully create a small dot, no bigger than the size of your iris, where you clear the frost. Then, at a distance exactly equivalent to the space between your pupils, place another small dot. Now you can put your face up to the glass to look at the outside world.

In a few moments, a drop of water may begin to trickle down the window from a dot. If a kid asks what that means, just say, "The window isn't really crying" even though it looks like it!

THE LAST HURRAH

This last entry is a time-honored sign of success. You'll hear it when things are going great with your nieces and nephews. Whether you're swinging them from their heels, playing hide-and-seek, or doing slight-of-hand magic, when you try to stop, they'll beg you to start all over.

"Again! Again!"

Hope to hear this refrain often and rejoice when you do.

EPILOGUE

We're in the crowded auditorium for the first-ever graduation ceremony of the Watershed School in Boulder, Colorado. And nobody expected this from Alice Porter.

Alice, the school's first graduating senior, was holding court. Composed and natural, poised and present as if she'd been doing this all her life, Alice was speaking to the whole school—parents, teachers, fellow students. She told about her time at Watershed School. And she was singling out people to thank.

Alice pulled out a vase of white roses and began calling individuals by name. She named some of her fellow students, thanked them specifically for the experiences they had given her, and handed each one a rose. She called out certain teachers and acknowledged the role they played in her time at Watershed. She gave each one of them a rose, too.

She called her mom to the front of the room, and while her mother made the self-conscious trek, Alice thanked her for those things she'd given her daughter. By now, the women in the audience are sniffling and even the men are blubbering. Her fellow students sat wide-eyed, amazed at the Alice who commands the room.

Then she called Tom, her father's brother, and asked him to come up front. Tom made the walk up the aisle, through the crowd, and stood beside Alice. He shifted his feet gently side to side, the seed of a smile on his face and the corners of his eyes crinkled.

Holding a white rose by its long stem, Alice said, "This rose is for Tom, my uncle. Tom was always there to say, 'Go do it.' Tom was always there to say, 'Alice, yes you can.' Tom was always there to say, 'Alice, you are a winner.' To give me encouragement. To help me learn that I can do anything I decide to do. And that's why I'm here today. And that's why I'm giving this rose to Uncle Tom today, on my graduation day."

By now, everyone in the audience has melted and the stock price of Kleenex has recorded a major uptrend. Everyone is sobbing, everyone except Alice and Tom.

Epilogue

The world needs more Alices. And to have them, we need more Toms. Toms who give encouragement to their Alices by saying, *"Yes, you can do it." "Yes, go out there and do it." "Yes, get to it." "Yes."*

And so I say to you, *"Yes. Get to it."*

ACKNOWLEDGMENTS

Thanks to Kelly Cash for giving me the initial encouragement to pursue this book. Thanks also to Cassius Harvey, Irish Harvey, Audrey Murray, Brittney Murray, and Jill Murray for testing and inventing many of these ideas, and to Michelle Ratola for the lessons she taught me. Larry Robertson provided needed advice and guidance. Margie Williams always gave her steady support. Thanks to Kris Lathrop for his artistic talent and to Barbara McNichol for her editorial guidance. Thanks also to Margo Toulouse at Morgan James Publishing for bringing this idea to reality.

ABOUT THE AUTHOR

Will Murray has 15 (that's *fifteen*, XV) nieces and nephews and no children, which makes him all uncle. He believes our society needs the kind of kids who grow up strong from being around great aunts and uncles. Will works with conservation organizations, climbs mountain peaks, fishes for trout, and participates in triathlons. He lives in Boulder, Colorado, with his wife, Margie Williams. They have no dogs.

ABOUT THE ILLUSTRATOR

Kris Lathrop has five new nieces and nephews and seven aunts and uncles of his own. Being with the nieces and nephews is his one chance to be a kid again. Kris currently lives in Boulder, CO and works in the solar industry. He is an avid cyclist, skier, and mountain climber who travels all over the world.

BUY A SHARE OF THE FUTURE IN YOUR COMMUNITY

These certificates make great holiday, graduation and birthday gifts that can be personalized with the recipient's name. The cost of one S.H.A.R.E. or one square foot is $54.17. The personalized certificate is suitable for framing and will state the number of shares purchased and the amount of each share, as well as the recipient's name. The home that you participate in "building" will last for many years and will continue to grow in value.

Here is a sample SHARE certificate:

HABITAT FOR HUMANITY

THIS CERTIFIES THAT

YOUR NAME HERE

HAS INVESTED IN A HOME FOR A DESERVING FAMILY

1985-2010

TWENTY-FIVE YEARS OF BUILDING FUTURES
IN OUR COMMUNITY ONE HOME AT A TIME

1200 SQUARE FOOT HOUSE @ $65,000 = $54.17 PER SQUARE FOOT
This certificate represents a tax deductible donation. It has no cash value.

YES, I WOULD LIKE TO HELP!

I support the work that Habitat for Humanity does and I want to be part of the excitement! As a donor, I will receive periodic updates on your construction activities but, more importantly, I know my gift will help a family in our community realize the dream of homeownership. **I would like to SHARE in your efforts against substandard housing in my community!** *(Please print below)*

PLEASE SEND ME _____ SHARES at $54.17 EACH = $ $_____

In Honor Of: _____

Occasion: (Circle One)   HOLIDAY   BIRTHDAY   ANNIVERSARY

    OTHER: _____

Address of Recipient: _____

Gift From: _____ *Donor Address:* _____

Donor Email: _____

I AM ENCLOSING A CHECK FOR $ $_____ **PAYABLE TO HABITAT FOR HUMANITY OR PLEASE CHARGE MY VISA OR MASTERCARD** *(CIRCLE ONE)*

Card Number _____ Expiration Date: _____

Name as it appears on Credit Card _____ Charge Amount $ _____

Signature _____

Billing Address _____

Telephone # Day _____ Eve _____

PLEASE NOTE: Your contribution is tax-deductible to the fullest extent allowed by law.
Habitat for Humanity • P.O. Box 1443 • Newport News, VA 23601 • 757-596-5553
www.HelpHabitatforHumanity.org